Animal Look-Alikes

Porcupines and Hedgehogs

Joanne Mattern

RED
CHAIR
·PRESS·

Animal Look-Alikes is produced and published by Red Chair Press:

Red Chair Press LLC   PO Box 333   South Egremont, MA 01258-0333

www.redchairpress.com

About the Author

Joanne Mattern is the author of nearly 350 books for children and teens. She began writing when she was a little girl and just never stopped! Joanne loves nonfiction because she enjoys bringing science topics to life and showing young readers that nonfiction is full of compelling stories! Joanne lives in the Hudson Valley of New York State with her husband, four children, and several pets, which look nothing alike!

Publisher's Cataloging-In-Publication Data

Names: Mattern, Joanne, 1963-

Title: Porcupines and hedgehogs / Joanne Mattern.

Description: [South Egremont, Massachusetts] : Red Chair Press, [2018] | Series: Animal look-alikes | Interest age level: 006-010. | Includes science vocabulary, fun facts, and trivia about each type of animal. | "Core content library." | Includes bibliographical references. | Summary: "Quills or spines. Pets or pests. Is it a porcupine or a hedgehog? Look inside to learn how these spiky mammals are alike and how they differ."--Provided by publisher.

Identifiers: LCCN 2016947287 | ISBN 978-1-63440-213-2 (library hardcover) | ISBN 978-1-63440-218-7 (ebook)

Subjects: LCSH: Porcupines--Juvenile literature. | Hedgehogs--Juvenile literature. | CYAC: Porcupines. | Hedgehogs.

Classification: LCC QL737.R652 M38 2018 (print) | LCC QL737.R652 (ebook) | DDC 599.35/97--dc23

Illustrations by Tim Haggerty.

Map illustrations by Joe LeMonnier.

Photo credits: Shutterstock except for the following: p. 13: Dreamstime; p. 8: Minden Pictures.

Printed in Canada

102017 1P FRNS18

Table of Contents

Porcupine or Hedgehog?

You see an animal with spikes on its back. Is it a porcupine? Or is it a hedgehog? These animals look alike, but they are not the same! Many people have trouble telling porcupines and hedgehogs apart, but it is easy if you know what to look for. Even though they are the same in some ways, in other ways they are very different. Let's find out more about these spiky animals!

Spiky Mammals

Both porcupines and hedgehogs are part of an animal group called **mammals**. Mammals have a backbone and are covered with hair or fur. Most mammals give birth to live babies. Baby mammals cannot take care of themselves. Instead, their mothers protect them. Female mammals also **nurse** their babies with milk from their bodies.

All mammals are warm-blooded. Mammals can control their body temperature. Their bodies stay the same temperature no matter what the temperature is around them. This is different from cold-blooded animals, like reptiles and amphibians.

North American porcupine showing teeth

NOW YOU KNOW!

Incisors keep growing throughout the animal's life. Rodents have to keep chewing on things to wear down their teeth to the right size.

Porcupines are part of a group of mammals called **rodents**. Rodents have very long, sharp front teeth in their top and bottom jaws. These teeth are called **incisors**. Squirrels, mice, hamsters, and beavers are also rodents.

Hedgehogs are not rodents. They are part of a different family. So even though hedgehogs and porcupines are the same in some ways, they are not part of the same animal family at all.

Hair and Quills

All mammals have fur or hair. A porcupine is covered with long hair. A layer of **quills** lies on top of the hair. Porcupines have more than 30,000 of these long, sharp quills. These quills are the number one way a porcupine protects itself. When a **predator** attacks, the porcupine shakes its quills. The quills fall off and stick into the predator. Quills are sharp and cause a lot of pain, so the predator usually leaves the porcupine alone.

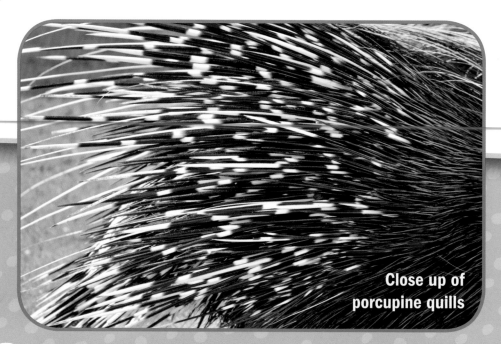

Close up of porcupine quills

Hedgehogs are also spiky, but they do not have quills. Instead, a hedgehog's **spines** are made of hair and **keratin**. Keratin is the hard material that makes up your fingernails. A hedgehog can have up to 7,000 spines.

When a predator comes close, a hedgehog rolls up into a spiky ball that is very hard to bite. These spines also protect hedgehogs from bumps and falls. It's like wearing a coat of spiky armor!

Now You Know!

When a porcupine loses its quills, it just grows new ones. A hedgehog's spines do not come off.

Big and Small

Another way to tell porcupines and hedgehogs apart is their size. Porcupines are much bigger than hedgehogs. The African porcupine is one of the largest. This porcupine is about three feet (1 m) long and can weigh up to 44 pounds (20 kg). North American porcupines are also very large. The smallest porcupine lives in South America. It is just a foot (30 cm) long and weighs about two pounds (9 kg).

Most porcupines are large and have sturdy bodies and short legs. However, some species have long tails. Long-tailed porcupines are thinner than other porcupines.

Compared to a porcupine, a hedgehog is tiny! Hedgehogs are only five to 12 inches (13–30 cm) long. They weigh between one and three pounds (0.5 to 1.3 kg).

African crested porcupines

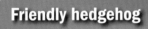

Friendly hedgehog

Different Species

There are 23 species of porcupines. Porcupines are divided into two groups. New World porcupines live in North America and South America. Old World porcupines live in Europe, Asia, and parts of Africa.

North African crested porcupine

There are also different kinds of hedgehogs. Hedgehogs can be divided into 14 species. These species live in Europe, Africa, and Asia. There are no native wild hedgehogs in North America, South America, or Australia.

Power Word: A species is a group of living things with the same features. The word can be singular or plural. These *species are* both spikey.

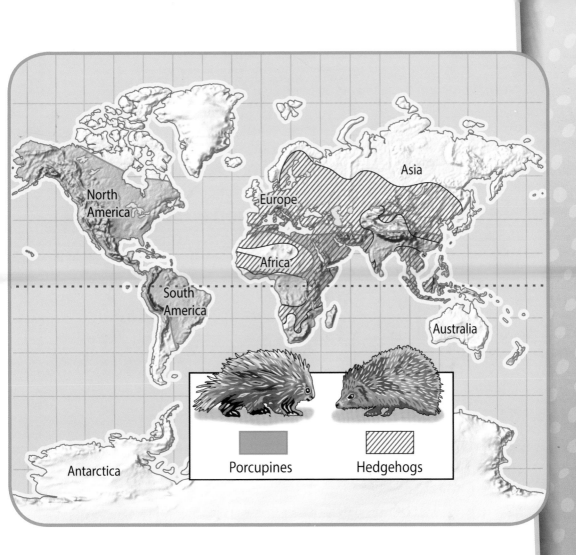

Porcupines	Hedgehogs

Now You Know!

All species of porcupines and hedgehogs are **nocturnal**, or active only at night.

Where Do You Call Home?

Porcupines live in many different **habitats**. Old World porcupines in Asia and Africa live on the ground. They can live in dry, hot areas, and also in cold places.

Brazilian porcupine

New World porcupines are **arboreal**. They live in trees. South American porcupines live in thick forests. North American porcupines live in forests and woods. Arboreal porcupines have wide feet and sharp claws to help them climb trees. Thin ridges on the bottom of their feet help them grip the bark.

Some porcupines prefer wooded areas and climb trees.

Tails can also help porcupines climb. The North American porcupine uses its hairy tail to grip the branch. South American porcupines have a long tail that can curl around branches.

Porcupines spend time on the ground too. They move along slowly on their short legs up to 20 miles (32 km) an hour.

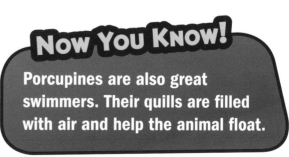

NOW YOU KNOW!

Porcupines are also great swimmers. Their quills are filled with air and help the animal float.

Hedgehogs also live in many different places. Some live in woods and forests. Others live in fields and farmlands. Many people in Europe find hedgehogs living in their gardens and yards. Some hedgehogs even live near the beach. Hedgehogs cannot climb trees, but they often hide under bushes.

Some people keep hedgehogs inside their houses. These animals can make good pets. But you would not want a porcupine as a pet!

Pet hedgehogs can be
fun to raise and nurture

A North American porcupine munching on a tree branch

European hedgehog in a garden

Different Diets

Porcupines and hedgehogs do not eat the same things. Porcupines are **herbivores**. They only eat plants. Leaves, flowers, grass, nuts, berries, and seeds are all tasty foods to a porcupine. Porcupines also love to chew on tree bark. A porcupine can chew so much bark off a branch that it breaks and falls down. Bark not only tastes good, but chewing on it helps wear down the porcupine's long front teeth.

Hedgehogs are **omnivores**, which means they eat both meat and plants. Hedgehogs dig in the ground to find worms and insects to eat. They will even eat small mice, frogs, and baby birds! Hedgehogs also eat fruit and mushrooms.

Now You Know!

Porcupines love salt. Human sweat contains salt. Porcupines will eat tool handles, shoes, and objects that people have touched just to get the salt left behind.

Prickly Babies

Female porcupines give birth to one baby at a time. A baby porcupine is called a porcupette. A porcupette can see and hear right after birth. It is covered with hair and soft quills. These quills harden a few hours after birth.

Mother porcupines nurse their babies and keep them safe from predators. They also teach them how to climb trees.

Hedgehogs have four or five babies in a **litter**. A baby hedgehog is called a hoglet. A female hedgehog can have one or two litters a year. Hedgehogs have soft, short spines when they are born. A few weeks later, they grow lots of hard spines.

Newborn hedgehog

Mother hedgehog
with babies

A North American porcupine
mother and baby rub noses

**Porcupine in winter
snow and cold**

What About Winter?

Some hedgehogs **hibernate** during the winter. Hedgehogs that live in cold places make a nest out of sticks, leaves, and grass. They snuggle into them to sleep all winter. They also eat plenty of food before they hibernate so they can get through the winter without eating.

Porcupines do not hibernate. They do not have any trouble finding food to eat during the winter. Tree branches and pine needles provide food all year long. A porcupine's thick fur also helps it keep warm during the winter months.

Meet the Echidna

Porcupines and hedgehogs are not the only spiky animals. The echidna is an animal that lives in Australia, Tasmania, and New Guinea. They make their homes in mountains, deserts, and forests.

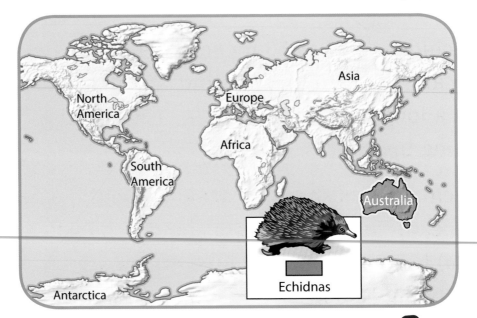

Asia

Europe

North America

Africa

South America

Australia

Antarctica

Echidnas

The echidna is one of only two mammals that lays eggs. A newborn echidna stays in a pouch in its mother's body until it grows spines about three months later.

Echidna

An echidna is 12 to 35 inches (30–89 cm) long and can weigh up to 35 pounds (16 kg). They have a long, thin snout that is perfect for sucking up insects.

An echidna has sharp spines on its back, sides, and head. These spines are about two inches (5 cm) long. When an echidna gets scared, it quickly digs a hole with its long, sharp claws. Then it jumps in so only its spines stick out. It is hard for a predator to grab this spiky ball, so the echidna is safe.

Protecting the Prickly

In the past, porcupines were an important source of food. Many North American settlers hunted them. Native Americans also hunted porcupines and used their quills and tails to make tools. During the 1900s, there were so many porcupines that the government paid people to hunt them. The timber industry also killed porcupines because they damaged trees. Today, most porcupines are no longer hunted or killed on purpose. This species is not **endangered**.

Hedgehogs, however, are in trouble in some parts of the world. In Great Britain, hedgehogs are an endangered species. Dry weather means there are fewer insects for them to eat. Hedgehogs also lose habitat when people build new roads, houses, or parking lots. People are working to save the hedgehog and make sure this cute, spiky animal is around for a long time.

Part of Our World

Porcupines and hedgehogs are important parts of our world. People once thought that porcupines damaged trees. Today we know that they help nature. When porcupines chew on tree leaves and branches, they allow more sunshine to strike the forest floor. They also clear dead wood from trees. Other animals can eat or make shelters out of the branches that fall to the ground.

Hedgehogs are helpful because they eat harmful insects. They are also friendly and make good pets. These animals are the same in some ways, but they are very different in others! Porcupines and hedgehogs—and echidnas too!—are important parts of our planet.

Baby porcupine in a tree

Glossary

arboreal living in trees

endangered in danger of dying out

habitats the natural place where animals and plants live

herbivores animals that only eat plants

hibernate to sleep deeply during the winter

incisors long, sharp front teeth

keratin a hard material found in hair and claws

litter a group of babies born at the same time

mammals animals that have backbones, fur or hair, are warm-blooded, and give birth to live young

nocturnal active at night

nurse to feed a baby with milk from the mother's body

ominvores animals that eat both plants and meat

predator an animal that hunts other animals for food

quills sharp spines that cover a porcupine's body

rodents animals that have long, sharp front teeth

spines hard spikes found on hedgehogs and echidnas

Read More in the Library

Rockwood, Leigh. *Tell Me the Difference Between a Porcupine and a Hedgehog.* Powerkids Press, 2013.